God Knows YOU

written by Elizabeth Elaine Watson

illustrated by Susan Edison

© 1981, The STANDARD PUBLISHING COMPANY, Cincinnati, Ohio
Division of STANDEX INTERNATIONAL CORPORATION   Printed in U.S.A.

God knows the leaves
that fall from a tree,

He knows the fish
that swim in the sea.

God knows every drop
of the falling rain,

 And wonder of all,
God knows your name.

God knows your face,
your frown and your smile,

He knows your tears
when you're sad for a while.

He knows each finger
you have on your hand,

He knows each toe
you wiggle in the sand.

God knows your eyes
that see the sun,

He knows your feet
that like to run.

God knows your voice
and the words you say,

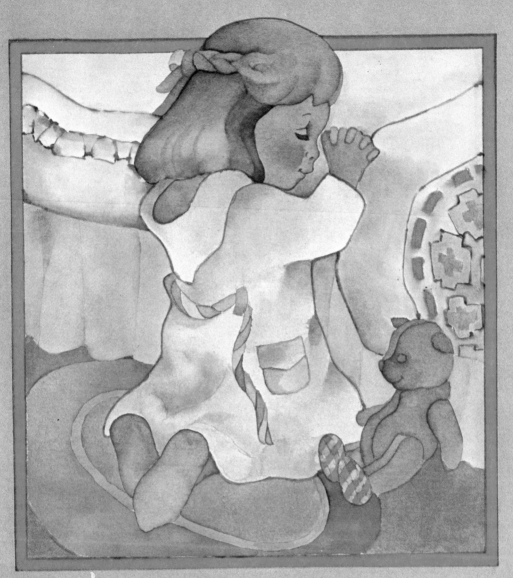

He knows your thoughts
when you bow to pray.

 God knows the footsteps
you take each day,

He knows your laughter
when you go to play.

He knows your hands
that help your mother,

And share your toys
with your baby brother.

 God knows where you live,
the name of your street,

He knows your room
and the bed where you sleep.

 God knows when you run
and play by the sea,

 He knows when you fall
and hurt your knee.

 God knows when you sleep
in your bed at night,

 He knows when you wake
in the morning light.

God knows you each day
from head to toe,
And wonder of all,
God loves you so.